Band of Hope & Glory

Mary Dennison

New Wine Press

New Wine Press
PO Box 17
Chichester
England PO20 6YB
England

Copyright © 1999 Mary Dennison

All rights reserved. No part of this publication may be reproduced, stored in a retrieval system, or transmitted in any form or by any means, electronic, mechanical, photocopying or otherwise, without the prior written consent of the publisher.

Short extracts may be used for review purposes.

All Scripture quotations are taken from the HOLY BIBLE, NEW INTERNATIONAL VERSION. Copyright © 1973, 1978, 1984 by International Bible Society. Used by permission.

THE MESSAGE – Eugene H. Peterson, published by NavPress Publishing Group, PO Box 35001, Colorado Springs, Colorado 80935.

ISBN: 1 874367 91 4

Illustrations by Katy Harrison.
Typeset by CRB Associates, Reepham, Norfolk.
Printed in England by Clays Ltd, St Ives plc.

Dedication

In memory of my much loved Dad, who never had any worldly wealth, but if riches could be measured by the love and esteem in which someone is held, he died one of the richest men in the world.

Acknowledgements

Mum – Thanks for everything ... the years of hard work raising your family ... the unconditional love which has kept us close – you're the best.

To all my brothers and sisters – it's smashing being a part of such a large and loving tribe.

Members of 'The Bridge Church' – for allowing me to dream and helping some of them to come true ... thank you – everything was tried and tested on you first ... sorry!

Mike and Margaret Pusey ... without your friendship I wouldn't laugh as much – I've seen Jesus in you.

My many friends, too numerous to name, who over the years have shaped my Christian life and permitted me to make the mistakes that I have ... you're remembered and appreciated.

And most especially ... to Paul, my super husband and best friend who knows all there is to know about me and loves me anyway ... our children Matthew and his wife Steph, Esther and husband Paul, Hannah and her boyfriend Mark – the ones that make life fun ... you're all very special, I love you loads.

Foreword

Knowing the Dennison family in friendship for many years has meant that hearing poetry recited by Mary after a good meal at their table, or as part of the programme at a church meeting at which I was to speak, has never failed to be a pleasurable experience.

Mary is quick to gather up occurrences from every day life and to form them into her own inimitable brand of poetry.

We have all met the people she portrays and have wished we could have 'painted them with our words'. Sometimes uncomfortably, but with a smile, we have been reminded of ourselves in certain circumstances and that has caused us to laugh – or blush! Not only are the poems enjoyable but the story behind their inspiration makes a good read.

Mary has a way of expressing the life that she and her husband Paul have enjoyed in Jesus Christ for many years. Life that is thoroughly naturally supernatural and earthed. A life that takes God really seriously but at the same time refuses to take others or even oneself too seriously at all!

It is time for some of these great poems to be published, it might have happened some years ago, but I am sure that it is meant 'for such a time as this'.

Mike Pusey
Itinerant Minister
Former Senior Pastor
'The King's Church'
Aldershot

Contents

	Foreword	7
	Introduction	11
1	'This Is God. Please Leave Your Message After The Tone!'	13
	Poem: *Next!*	17
2	I Don't Wish To Split Hairs God, But...	19
	Poem: *Hair Today – Gone Tomorrow*	22
3	Pride Cometh Before A Fall	25
4	Six Days Shalt Thou Labour ... And On The Seventh?	28
	Poem: *Band Of Hope & Glory!*	34
5	Running The Race	38
	Poem: *My New Year's Resolution – I'm Giving It Up*	41
6	Be Sure Your Sins Will Find You Out	44
	Poem: *The Great And The Small*	48
7	Great Expectations	49
	Poem: *I Expect*	52
8	Gone To War – Back In An Hour	55
	Poem: *Sideways Christian Soldiers*	57
9	Now Is The Time For All Good Men To Come To The Aid Of The Party	60
	Poem: *For Pity's Sake!*	64

10	**This Is A Government Health Warning**	67
	Poem: ***There's One More Annie In Heaven***	71
11	**Spiritual DIY**	74
	Poem: ***Interior Decoration***	77
12	**Ruling Together**	79
	Poem: ***Woe-Man***	82
13	**Go Ahead Caller – You're Through**	86
	Poem: ***Here I Am Lord – Send Him***	89
14	**A Final Word**	92

Introduction

My name is Mary Dennison – **the** Mary Dennison. Well, there's only one as far as I'm aware.

'I've never heard of you' will be your quick riposte, and you'd be right. Not that it matters in the least that you've never heard of me, but my aim is that after reading this book, you should know a little bit about me. Why, you're asking, should you want to do that? Writing this introduction on a blank page and with a mind to match, I wish I could conjure up a reasonable inducement for so doing. Let me explain...

I have endeavoured over a number of years to entertain people through 'An Evening with Mary' – an evening designed to introduce people to my friend. You see, **everyone** has **heard** of my friend, even if they haven't heard of me, but some of the people I have in my audiences don't really **know** him.

God is like that. To most people, he is a mystery to be unravelled, rather than an awesome, all-powerful, loving, compassionate Father to be known. Because God wants us to know him, he created a way through his Son Jesus.

As I've listened to people over many years talk of their doubts and misgivings regarding Christianity, I've wanted to communicate some answers. One of the ways I chose to do that was through poetry.

No ... don't go ... come back, please ... I knew that word might put you off!

When performing the poetry I seek to inject some humour and excitement into it, believing this to be preferable to a tedious recital of words, because God has both these qualities. Following these evenings, people have asked if I have written a book, as they would like to have one. The first few who said it flattered me. Actually I was still in a state of being flattered when a few more had said it too. Instead of repenting (too much pride being a sin, and when humble I'm usually proud of it), I decided to do just that. Visions of rejection slips dogged my attempts at regular intervals, but I pressed on regardless.

I'm told I'm very down to earth, therefore this is not a book designed to explore deep theological truths aimed at theologians. So that might well commend it!

Through the following pages, I'll give you a warts 'n' all whistle-stop tour through my life as a Christian. But more importantly, I hope to introduce you to a loving Father God, my friend and Saviour Jesus, and because he lives in me and is part of me, the Holy Spirit.

Mary Dennison
1999

1

'This Is God. Please Leave Your Message After The Tone!'

People think Christians are boring.

I've been one, not a bore that is, but a Christian, for as many years as Jesus lived on earth, so that must earn me a few Brownie points. Yet, I openly confess that I find the above impression still has more than a tad of truth to it. Since my dictionary tells me that a bore will 'weary by tedious talk or dullness', I'll be mortified if after reading this book you are fully convinced of my opening statement.

I like talking. The most common cause for relationships breaking down, I'm told, is people not being able to talk to one another. My husband rather needlessly points out that he would be fully stretched to **imagine** a scenario where we had such difficulty! We live in an era of communication technology as we've never known before, with telephones, faxes, e-mail, satellites, and much more. But have we perhaps lost the uncomplicated, yet rewarding art of what used to be **ordinary** conversation – talking to one another, face to face?

My brother Marty is a partner in a building firm, and I used to work for him on a part-time basis. The office was unoccupied for most of the day, hence an answerphone had been installed, and in the morning my first task was to make a note of the messages. Normally articulate people would suddenly become confused, tongue-tied, inarticulate gibbering wrecks when confronted with talking to a machine. I identify with their difficulty, because I had quite a flustering experience when a new car-park opened in my district some years ago. Up until this time, I had rather quaintly been used to paying a man in a ticket booth, positioned at the car-park exit. It all seemed so simple, yet strangely it worked. But now technology had arrived.

The new car-park required you to pay at the machine **before** returning to your car, **before** exiting.

I didn't know that.

Consequently, when I returned to the car park, I had almost driven away before remembering the newfangled machine. Driving back, I headed off hastily towards the **'PAY HERE'** sign and then frustratingly discovered that I didn't have any change for the aforementioned machine. Whilst I stood there in exasperation, suddenly, a host of angels appeared.

'Fear not!' they said.

No they didn't, but I **did** hear a disembodied voice say, 'have you got a problem?'

Could this be God?

Unlikely, as it was coming from the ticket machine. I looked around, expecting any minute to see Jeremy Beadle approaching. Convinced I'd been had, I prepared for celebrity. However, the only man in the immediate vicinity didn't look anything like Jeremy Beadle, or the slightest bit interested in me, so I discounted that theory also. Once more, I heard the 'voice' ask, 'do you have a problem?', whereupon I tentatively inched closer to the machine, and explained that indeed I did. I felt such a fool speaking to the machine, and prayed to the invisible God that no-one was watching me. In those few enlightening moments I discovered that not only could machines be very helpful, but they could flirt with you too, as this one was doing – outrageously.

How was I to know that I was on CCTV and the entertainment was being enjoyed by the 'voice' and numerous men in the downstairs office!

I was extremely amused therefore, by this particular message left on my brother's office answerphone.

'B*!!** answerphone.' Sound of phone being slammed down.

Next attempt the caller is obviously determined not to be brow-beaten by the technological barrier between him and the intended recipients of his message, and he managed to complete his message quite succinctly, which was...

'B*!!** Builders.'

Quite!

Another time, another caller was this time taken aback by my answering the phone with a cheery 'Good morning!'

'Hello,' he said.

I responded, 'Good morning, Ian Smith Builders.'

His tone now a little more tentative and questioning. He said, 'hello' once more.

'How may I help you?' I enquired.

'Am I talking to the machine?' was his bewildered response.

Eventually, I was able to reassure this perplexed customer that he had, by chance, stumbled upon one of those **rare** moments when he was actually speaking to a human being.

Jockeying for position at the top of the *'Stressful Experience'* list can be a visit to the GP. One needs to gird one's ailing loins from the outset, as there's the receptionist to get past.

Here's a handy hint.

Book yourself onto a ten-week course entitled 'How To Be Assertive' **before** you feel ill. Helps enormously. Triumphing in difficult circumstances by getting an appointment, could be the reason why, as I have found, one **immediately** starts to feel better! A rush of adrenaline maybe? Once in front of the doctor, have you found yourself babbling off your, by now, fading ailments? None of us wishes to be considered a time-waster, thus if the look on our GP's face doesn't register enthralment by our every word, we interpret it as lack of interest and care. Before you can say antibiotics, you're out of the door with a prescription to obtain some. Sound familiar?

How much easier it is to talk to someone properly, including our much maligned doctors, to take time to get to know them, to build up confidence and trust. But time is of the essence in our over-stretched Health Service, and most doctors provide an excellent service despite the constraints upon them.

I used to be daunted at the thought of praying. Prayer is simply conversation with God, and like all good conversations must be two-way, with time being taken to **listen** also. We all pray far more than we think we do, and nearly everyone has called upon God at some crisis point in their lives, whether professing to believe in him or not.

But is he interested? Is he listening?

I believe he **is** and **does**, and I'm positive he has never shouted, *'Next!'*

Next!

Patient: 'Oh Doctor, Good Morning, I've come to tell
What's currently ailin' me.
I've got a chronic dose of...

Doctor: 'Can I have your *name* please.'

Patient: ...heartburn, so painful when I drink tea.'

Doctor: 'Right, Mrs Heartburn, now what are your symptoms?
I haven't *all day* you know
So take a deep breath and tell me what's wrong
When I give you a nod and say "go!"'

Patient: 'Well ... I really don't like to bovver you
You know I'm 'ardly ever 'ere...'

Doctor: 'Your ear you say – I'll take a look
Ears can be dodgy things
You really don't want earache
I know the pain it brings...

It looks OK there's nothing wrong
It's not the *least* bit pink
I might be *rude* in saying this
But you're wasting my time I think.'

Patient: 'No, it's *not* my *ear*, now 'ave an 'eart
I'm trying to be quick...'

Doctor: 'So – it's *not* your ear, now it's your *heart* that's quickening
What a *changing* situation
It's really nothing serious
Just a minor palpitation.'

Patient: 'Now listen to me, my 'eart's alright
I'm not about to die
And you'd better pay attention
If we're to see eye to eye.'

Doctor: 'Yes, I noticed the minute you walked in
That you seemed to have a slight squint
But this is the *Doctors'* and not the *Opticians'*
And I do wish you'd take the hint
For wasting time is not allowed... on the NHS!'

Patient: 'Now look 'ere Doc, is this some kind of joke?
'Cos you need takin' down a peg
But p'raps it's just your bit of fun
In which case...
Pull the other leg!'

Doctor: 'Hmm ... your legs are quite bandy
I noticed that at first glance
Supportive panty hose *might* help
But your *looks* they won't enhance.
So, let's sum up the situation shall we
See where we've got so far
You've palpitations, bandy legs and a squint
and an earache ... possibly caused by catarrh.'

Patient: 'Right, that's it. I've had enough
Are you some kind of quack?
I'm leavin' now, and I *guarantee*
I won't be comin' back
I'll make a note of your name
So you in the future I can avoid
And one more thing before I go
Me name's not *'eartburn*, it's
Emma Roid!!'

2

I Don't Wish
To Split Hairs God, But...

Put to the vote, were I to conduct an 'Exit Poll' as people leave church on a Sunday, I'm pretty certain God would not fare very well to the question –

'Do you think God **likes** you?'

He would fare even less well in the answers from those who purport to be agnostic, and I guess the question would be altogether irrelevant to an atheist.

My niece Katy is a lovely girl, and it is she who has drawn the comic illustrations for this book. She had real character as a toddler, which has developed into a wonderful sense of humour as an adult. When trying to convince people that God not only **likes** them, but **loves** them, I frequently draw upon an incident from Katy's childhood to illustrate my point.

One day Katy had been naughty, and therefore duly chastised for her misdemeanour. In this two-year-old's opinion the ticking off had been entirely unjustified, and so she had gone off muttering to herself under her breath. Upon asking her what she was saying, my sister got this reply.

'I'm telling Jesus about you.'

'What are you telling him?' enquired her mother.

'That I don't like you very much.'

'And what is he saying to that?'

'He says that **he** doesn't like you very much either!'

Funny, yet it hits the proverbial nail right on the head when it comes to stating what we often believe...

God doesn't like us!

In fact, he's out to get us, pointing the finger, not looking down simply figuratively from heaven, but looking down on us full stop.

The Bible tells us over and over how much God loves us, **John 3:16** being the definitive example:

> *'For God so loved the world, that he gave his one and only Son, that whoever believes in him shall not perish but have eternal life.'* (NIV)

Psalm 139 says *'you knit me together in my mother's womb'*, and **Matthew 10** informs that *'even the very hairs on your head are numbered'*.

Still not convinced?

Neither was I as a teenager. If God was going to go to all the trouble of **counting** my hairs, the very least he could have done would be to make sure that I had a few **straight** ones! I have naturally wavy hair ... now. As a teenager it was naturally frizzy (although I've since discovered it's not natural at all, it's a sign of diseased roots).

'Oh what lovely hair,' I was constantly told by the older generation ... (at that time, anyone over 30), whilst feeling at liberty to push and poke my profusion of corrugated locks.

Surely God, if he **existed**, must **know** that to be **cool**, groovy and **in**, in the 60s meant having **dead straight** hair with not a kink in sight (other than the band, that is). I was in the wrong era, born too early or too late, and God was not to be easily forgiven.

With my self-esteem at rock bottom, I wholeheartedly believed that my life would be transformed by the addition of straight hair.

It couldn't, and it wasn't.

In the 70s and 80s, all varieties of hair types became acceptable. There was punk, spiky, straight and curly. Some, including my husband, would have counted themselves fortunate indeed to have hair of any persuasion or hue. But in the politically correct 90s, being follicly challenged (formerly known as baldness) is fashionable, and more and more men (and some women) **purposefully** shave their heads to be ahead in the fashion stakes.

Magazines, television and the media in general, constantly

bombard us with the latest trends, and images of how we **should** look to be acceptable in a society obsessed with the body beautiful. I enjoy (and as a Christian it is OK to) being fashionable and looking the best that I can. In the ordinary peoples' 'Top 100 worst-dressed persons' awards', Christians have been generally hailed as the outright winners, without resistance from outsiders. It is a dubious honour some still like to preserve. Having said that, I'm also aware of how much more important the **inside** of us is, especially to God. He looks here to find the **real** person.

I feel privileged to have grown up in a very large family, but being the youngest in a family of nine children didn't afford me much privacy. In our experience, **alone** meant something other people got when they borrowed money. I say other people because my parents had very little money, and never even had a bank account. Having one's own space was as rare as sleeping in one's own bed on one's own. So as a little girl, I decided to rectify this lack of solitude by moving all the furniture around to form a small den. Having achieved this, I climbed inside to stake my claim and proclaim to all around that this was **my territory**.

Some time elapsed before my sister felt forced to enquire as to what I was doing, as I had become inaudible. This was remarkably uncommon, thus setting alarm bells ringing.

With extreme annoyance at my sister's unwelcome intrusion, I retorted...

'Please don't look at me when I'm **changing** my mind!'

Something must have been going on in my young head that didn't warrant going public on – quite what, I can now only imagine. If others could see what was going on inside us, as well as seeing what we **want** them to see on the outside, I'm positive we would eagerly submit our lives to undergoing some transformation.

It would take far more than the acquisition of straight hair, as I was to discover.

But was it really **so** bad, still to want it?

Hair Today – Gone Tomorrow

(Imagine this poem recited with a Liverpool accent, as it is so reminiscent of the 60s.)

I want to take you back to the 60s
To the Beatles, The Stones and The Who
And a teenager called Mary
Who didn't know what to do
'Cos a mass of frizzy curls
Lay in confusion on 'er 'ead
Meaning every night she 'ad to wear
Hair curlers to 'er bed
The purpose not to curl 'er hair
'Cos the rollers were **Jumbo** size
But to straighten, to smooth and unkink it
So that 'er fringe could 'ang over 'er eyes
Instead of pathetically curled at the ends
Like a sarni from British Rail
And to make the transformation complete
She prayed for a face that was pastel and pale
Instead of the freckles and rosy cheeks that prevailed
Insistent upon 'er phizog
So instead of lookin' like Cilla Black or Lulu
She resembled Sally, the family dog!
Oh! to look like Cathy McGowan
With hair that was silky and straight
Instead of a demented Brillo Pad
So 'er curly hair she grew to hate
They called 'er Henry VIII at school
She'd rather have been Anne Bolyn
But that would 'ave been bordering on vanity
And that would 'ave been a *SIN*!!
She 'ated the days they 'ad PE
It meant in the shower she 'ad to go
And the steam used to make her hair *FRIZZ*
Which was worse than 'avin BO

I Don't Wish To Split Hairs God, But...

So the years they came and the years they went
And as they cheered the 70s in
Mary's hair at last was straighter
So the rollers went in the bin
But alas for poor Mary the moral was this
An 'ard lesson she 'ad to learn
'Cos now 'er hair was *lovely and straight*
But the fashion was a ***CURLY PERM***!!

3

Pride Cometh Before A Fall

...and fame goeth to the head! Well, it did for me one day, quite literally.

As I hadn't been captured in the car park by Jeremy Beadle after all, celebrity didn't come by that route. It did though, inasmuch as my picture appeared in a local newspaper, which being a freebie was designed to captivate the attention of every unsuspecting household in the neighbourhood where I live. Not long after the picture had appeared, I went shopping in the local supermarket. I still could ... without recognition! Having just washed and blow-dried my hair, I shall lay aside all false modesty and say it was looking sleek and rather splendid.

Entering the shop, I observed that one or two shoppers were giving me more than a cursory glance, but undeterred, and possibly somewhat flattered, I continued with my shopping. The attention also continued apace however ... actually following me up the aisle, and furthermore the 'follower' was a young woman who was a near neighbour. I caught her **obvious** attention and smiled. No warning bells clanged, even when I became aware that she had sadly developed a muscular twitch to her lips that I hadn't hitherto been aware of. Could it be my picture in the paper, I pondered, bringing me all this unexpected attention? Is this what it is like to be famous?

By now, I had joined the queue at the checkout. A confectionery rep was nearby stacking sweets in the very place that you don't want them to be when you have a small child in your trolley, as I did. Only in my desire to pay attention to detail shall I inform you that he was very good-looking, not for any other reason of course, and that he too was staring at me. Before becoming overwhelmed however, by the effect such flattery would have on my vanities, the look was followed by what can only be described as a suppressed laugh. Must be enjoying a private joke, I concluded. Anyhow, he's not **that** good-looking after all. Why then when I rode away on my old and rusty bike did I still have an inner disquiet that I **was** the object of his amusement? I had no time to dwell on this possibility because I had to collect my son Matthew, and daughter Esther from school. Arriving in good time with a few minutes to spare, I perched myself on the wall to enjoy the afternoon sunshine. Moments later I was aware of being tapped on the shoulder from behind, and slightly startled, turned to see the neighbour who had been watching me in the supermarket.

'I hope you don't mind me mentioning this' she said, somewhat apologetically, 'but did you know you've got two hair curlers in the back of your hair?'

My hand flew to my head to rid myself of the offending bright pink and yellow **Jumbo** monstrosities, required to **straighten**, not to **curl**! I **immediately** recalled putting them there, to beat into submission a particularly wayward section of hair that wouldn't be tamed by blow-drying, and chastised myself for being so forgetful.

Thoroughly humiliated by this incident, I vowed that it would **never**, **ever** happen again. A few months later I did exactly the same thing. However, this time, I allowed the people in the Doctor's surgery to enjoy the free entertainment.

The white flag of surrender has now been waved, and these days the back of my hair enjoys being wayward!

4

Six Days Shalt Thou Labour... And On The Seventh?

Most people go to church at some time in their life.
A notice I read outside a local church said this:

'When we are born our parents bring us to church to be christened. When we get older they bring us to get married. When we die our friends bring us to bury us – try coming on your own sometime!'

No such clever advertising existed when I was a child, but then our family didn't **go** to church, we practically **lived** there. Talk about Sunday being a day of rest – not in our house. We spent the entire day in overdrive.

For starters there was morning Sunday School, and considering we lived a mile or so from the church, as a little girl it was quite a walk there and back. My brothers would occasionally take me in the pushchair to conserve my energy, and like all children would get up to a number of pranks en route. One I recall is that they would frequently stop on the way, to leave me sitting outside what they thought was an empty house, vacated by a dead spinster. Nevertheless, I was asked to keep a look-out, just in case.

Being so young, I wasn't aware they'd gone apple scrumping, until one day when they were nobbled by the 'dead' spinster. With hindsight, she was more of a recluse than dead – but how were we to know! You have to be pretty quick-thinkers to survive in a family of nine, and my brothers Andy and Marty were at the front of the queue in this department. The spinster rebuked them for their 'crime', and initially threatened to call the police, but after they had exercised a bit of charm, something they were very adept at doing, her merciful side came to the fore, and she reduced the penalty to simply telling our parents. With innocent faces they gave an address some three miles from where we really lived, and then we hurried off to Sunday School.

After Sunday School came something more 'meaty' – the morning service, unbelievably dull through my young eyes. Whether my brothers repented that morning I can't be sure, but never mind, there would be another opportunity, as after a quick lunch (more meat), we were back to church for afternoon Sunday School. Obviously our souls needed yet more feeding, but as our bodies did as well it was home for tea to work up an appetite for the evening service. If conviction of sin was dragging its feet in my brothers hearts, this meeting was to afford them the day's final chance.

The services varied in length, but if there **was** any repenting still to be done I hoped it would be done **quickly**, in order for us to 'Beat the Clock' and be home in time for Bruce Forsyth and Sunday Night at the London Palladium.

Monday follows Sunday, and for us Monday meant one thing ... Band of Hope! For the uninitiated this was a dizzy mixture of learning about Jesus from Bible stories, playing games on the beach on fine days, and signing the Pledge! Not a tin of furniture polish, but a document stating our intention to abstain from alcohol for the rest of our lives. As a seven- or eight-year-old I would have found it quite easy to make such a promise. I was not aware then of the irony of being taught about Jesus turning 180 gallons of water into wine, in Band of Hope's environment of temperance! Since I enjoy a nice glass of red wine, it's probably just as well my mother had good sense and never encouraged us to sign until we were of an age to make an informed decision.

The piéce-de-resistance of Band of Hope had to be the Temperance Meeting. Here my interests were entirely focused on the Temperance Queen, as she arrived in an atmosphere of dignified solemnity, bedecked in her beautiful gown and cape. Thus my ambitions were fuelled to be 'it' one day. (I guess some ambitions aren't destined to be fulfilled.) There were flags and banners in abundance and lady sopranos warbled. I didn't have a clue what it was all about, but I loved it.

Trying to explain things to children, in order that they may understand, has taxed adults since Adam had a twinkle in his eye for Eve, and I was frequently confused about what went on at Sunday School, Church and Band of Hope. Stories have circulated in my family for years about our children's misunderstandings, and I still find them amusing.

Our daughter Esther had thoroughly enjoyed a poetry book that she had been reading, and upon finishing it declared 'Anon' to be her favourite poet. Names can be the source of difficulty in many ways as proven by our son Matthew. As a small boy he wrote to the popular TV programme 'Jim'll Fix It', addressing his letter to Dear Jim'll.

Be careful how you explain away some of the childhood myths, because as my sister was to discover, that too can be fraught with difficulty. Believing that her son Peter might be teased at school for still believing in the Tooth Fairy, she felt when his latest molar to become dislodged was excitably displayed, she ought to do some explaining. Choosing her words carefully, and not wishing to upset him, she divulged that it was Mummy who put the money under the pillow, not the fairies. Instead of the anticipated tears, a broad smile lit up his face with pleasure as he exclaimed, 'gosh Mummy, how do you manage to get round to all the houses?'

Even when the 'facts of life' are given straight, and euphemisms used sparingly, we can't always convince the young. Following his first sex education lesson at home, the same nephew disbelievingly retorted to my sister, 'oh yes, go on Mum, now tell me the truth!'

Christmas Nativity plays never fail to bring a lump to the throat, and most parents eagerly await the annual school production, wondering which part their child will be called upon to dramatically bring to life. Of course, if we're honest, the starring role has to be Mary, and mothers of daughters live in hope. However, my niece Joanne had ambitions to play quite a different role, which we did find perplexing when she first mooted it. Who on earth was Beverley Hem, the character she had set her sights on? Further explanation was obviously required.

'Beverley Hem rings the bells,' my niece professed, as a response to our failure to fully grasp her aspirations for this role. Seeing our still confused expressions she said somewhat exasperatedly, 'you know, in the song "Little Donkey" – ring out those bells tonight ... Beverley Hem!' An easy mistake to make I think you'd all agree.

Sometimes children say things which inadvertently arrive at the truth without any pretensions. Returning from what had been a rather boring, but short, Ecumenical meeting, my husband and I had been secretly rather pleased at its brevity. When our daughter Hannah innocently thanked God that night for the '**economical** meeting', we felt obliged to add a sincere 'Amen!'

Hannah is pretty gifted at saying it like it is, and some of her pronouncements as a little girl were unerring in their accuracy. Hearing me bemoan the circles under my eyes one morning she stated teasingly –

'They're not circles Mummy.'

I was somewhat reassured until she completed her sentence...

'They're semi-circles.'

However, I digress. I was telling you about Band of Hope and Sunday School as this is the topic of my next poem. I'm unshaken in my belief that my teachers did their very best to impart the stories of Jesus in a manner that was **relevant** at that time – **But** – much of it left me baffled. We sang songs in abundance, and understanding the lyrics didn't appear to be crucial to our enjoyment of them, any more than it is today.

My brother Andy was frequently mildly rebuked when singing a certain song called, 'The Disciples Went Out Fishing', which was accompanied by carefully 'choreographed' actions. The aim was to throw our nets into the sea in the first verse, thus depicting the Galilean tradition, and haul them in at the end of the song. This seemingly, was not the way Andy felt it was best demonstrated, and he would always cast in a modern-day fishing rod, and finish by reeling it in. The Superintendent was not overtly amused – but we were!

Of course, confusion is not the sole prerogative of children. Perhaps that is why Jesus taught **adults** too in parables, keeping things simple, yet profound.

On an embarrassment scale of 1–10, I consider the following incident in my life must rate a good 9. Childish misconceptions are one thing, but when they follow you into what should be the peak of your adolescence, it's quite different. Currently employed by a large computer company, I was one day singing quietly whilst sitting at my desk unaware that anyone else was paying attention. It was a song that I had heard on the television the previous evening, as we had sat enjoying the 'Last Night of The Proms', in those days one of my mother's favourite programmes. It transported me back to the days of my childhood, so reminiscent was it of 'Temperance Sunday' – the banners, the flags and not least the warbling sopranos.

A colleague who had been standing nearby, moved a little closer and appeared to listen more intently.

'What **are** you singing Mary?' he enquired.

'Oh ... Band of Hope and Glory' came my misconceived but nonetheless confident reply!

Six Days Shalt Thou Labour ... And On The Seventh? 33

Band Of Hope And Glory!

(The lines marked *Music* would normally be sung, but you'll have to imagine that for the purposes of the book.)

[*Music*]: **Do you want a Pilot? Signal then to Jesus...**

>Well, we all need someone in our life
>To guide and steer and lead us
>So come on Jesus, climb on board
>I'm raring now to go
>Pull the throttle out, full steam ahead
>Life's for living, not going slow
>What's this course you're taking?
>Have you learnt to navigate?
>This route doesn't agree with mine
>At this rate we'll be late
>And we'll miss all the action
>Over there is where it's at
>If this was a game of cricket
>I'd have someone else in bat
>But Jesus knows what's best for me
>I really should stay cool
>For God's in charge of my life
>They **told** me ... at Sunday School!

[*Music*]: **Jesus wants me for a Sunbeam**
To shine for him each day...

>I'll only sin a little bit
>When He turns the other way
>But it really is quite worrying
>'Cos I'm told that He can see
>All the evil, wicked nasty things
>That go on inside of me
>Jesus wants me for a Sunbeam
>A dynamic little ray
>Who in every way tries to please Him
>At home ... at school ... at play
>But I think my light is fading

I'm not feeling hot at all
I should pray now for forgiveness
They ***told*** me ... at Sunday School!

[*Music*]: **I'm H.A.P.P.Y.
I'm H.A.P.P.Y.**

I'm happy almost all the time
It's only when I weep ... that I cry!
But that's the way it should be
'Cos my cup is...

[*Music*]: **Running over, running over
My cup's full and running over, running over ...
running out...**

I think it's almost empty
What's this all about?
What's running over anyway?
I'm feeling like a fool
Singing words I don't understand
'Cos I ***learnt*** them ... at Sunday School!

[*Music*]: **Band Of Hope And Glory!**

[*Music*]: **Now Zacchaeus was a very little man
And a very little man was he
Would I still sing this silly song
If he'd been as tall as me
If he'd been as tall as me
Now when the Saviour passed that way
He looked into the tree
And He said ... 'Zacchaeus, The Price Is Right ...
So Come On Down!**
[*Music*]: **For I'm coming to your house for tea
I'm coming to your house for tea'**

**I will make you fishers of men
Fishers of men, fishers of men
I will make you fishers of men
If you'll follow me...**

The trouble you see with fishing
Is you've got to have some bait
Something to attract the fish
And make them want to eat
I've dangled this and I've dangled that
From my spiritual fishing line
And sometimes I've toiled for ages
And spent a lot of time
But when I've hauled my catch in
More often then not, I have to say
'I've not hooked my friend for Jesus yet
She's the one that got away.'
But standing firm, not giving in
Has been my golden rule
I learnt that from my teacher
Who ***taught*** me ... at Sunday School!

It wasn't all bad ... was it?
But it wasn't always good
It's only now I realise
That I never understood
But when it comes to words in song
Listen now to these
Directed at our Father
The one I aim to please

[*Music*]: **Father God I wonder**
How I managed to exist
Without the knowledge
     of your parenthood
And your loving care
But now I am your son
I am adopted in your family
And I can never be alone
'Cos Father God
     you're there beside me

I will sing your praises
I will sing your praises
I will sing your praises
For evermore

**I will sing your praises
I will sing your praises
I will sing your praises
For evermore.***

---

* Ishmael – Thankyou Music, PO Box 75, Eastbourne, East Sussex BN23 6NW, UK

5

Running The Race

Despite my quest to catch God's eye through my faithful commitment by practically taking up residence in my local church, it didn't apparently sway, dazzle, affect, persuade, entice, or convince those who know about these things to conclude that I was a Christian. Since by definition a Christian is a person 'believing in, professing, or belonging to Christ', it renders trying to inveigle your way in by any other route a non-starter. That's my paraphrase of **Jesus'** words in **John 14:6** when he says...

> *'I am the way, the truth and the life. No one comes to the Father except through me.'*

So the one and only way is to ask Jesus into your life as Lord and Saviour. This I did at the age of 15 when the well-known evangelist Billy Graham said '**I'm going to invite you to get up out of your seat**,' at his London Crusade in the 1960s. Making my way to the front of the huge crowd was the easy part, only later would I realise the impact my decision to commit my life to Jesus would have. Right now, I was fired with enthusiasm to be all out for God, and to go to **all** the church meetings, which I'd been led to believe were one and the same thing.

By now I was attending a Baptist church some 5 miles from my home. My sister Jean and her husband Mike had taken me along with them one day, and it appealed immediately because there were lots of teenagers present, and more importantly ... some very nice boys. When delving deeply and spiritually into where God wants you to worship, it's good to be totally **honest** with him about what your **priorities** are!

Being told that Christians needed a crutch to lean on, soon became a familiar accusation to me – the implication being that we were too weak to get through life on our own. The fact is, we **all** have a need of God – admitting it is a **strength**, rather than a weakness. Added to that, I once tried to use some crutches – they weren't at all easy to use and required a deal of patience to come to terms with, but perseverance brought results. I quickly discovered that living the Christian life was not easy and those who suggested otherwise had clearly lost the plot. I, and many others in the church at that time, had still to discover that Jesus came to give us **life** in abundance, not **meetings**. To give up, was a frequent temptation not easily resisted, and feelings of inadequacy and of letting God down could easily be succumbed to.

The standards we set ourselves, rather than the ones God sets us are often impossible to achieve. The more we try, the more we seem to fail. Why is it that most people appear to make New Year resolutions they're rarely able to keep? Mostly, they are a cathartic exercise full of good intentions, but lacking the tenacity to be carried through. Could it be for the reason that most people resolve to **give up** something, such as cigarettes, swearing, biting nails, and because they're made **after** Christmas, food and drink? I'm told nothing arouses more false hope than the first four hours of a diet! Without hope it is impossible to continue, hence so many failed dietary resolutions.

Friends too would be relinquished. Instead of affecting our friends with our new-found faith, they could often be neglected, as we allowed structures to override the importance of people and relationships.

Isn't it encouraging therefore that God isn't like us ... fickle. The Bible says that *'God does not change'* (Malachi 3:6). In other words he is consistent. Whilst we're trying hard to succeed, he resolutely will not give up on us, even in our failure.

I frequently threatened to leave home as a child. Being the youngest of nine children I felt I had my work cut out in gaining a platform for my opinions. When I failed to impress, and the going was getting tough, it was time I felt for the tough to get going. When no more than 7 or 8 years old I announced my departure in grand style, insisting that no-one try and stop me – my mind was made up.

The council estate where I lived at the time formed a circle, and in the middle was the village green. Leaving the house with a retort of **'you'll miss me when I'm gone,'** I strutted off down the road with as much dignity as I could muster.

The only trouble I now found presenting itself was, once you've slammed the door on your old life and made a grand exit, it's downhill, metaphorically speaking, all the way. I was experiencing something of an anti-climax.

What now? Where does a 7–8-year-old go?

Well, this one decided to walk around the village green – endlessly. And did the family make it any easier? Did they heck! They would wave at me every time I passed the house, as averting my eyes, I pretended not to notice them smiling at the window.

Eventually I would admit to myself what I'd known from the outset – that walking round the block is an over-rated pastime. The comforts of home, which a while ago I'd been eager to abandon, were beckoning. Just one difficulty to overcome – how to save face?

Got it!

Off home, determination now in my steps, I flung open the door to my bemused parents and siblings to declare...

'I'm going to give you all **one** more chance!'

My New Year's Resolution – I'm Giving It Up

Today, I gave my life to Jesus
What a crazy thing to do
But I took at look at my life
And I hankered for something new
The bloke said at the rally
Which was where this all took place
That once you were a Christian
You were running in a race
Not looking back behind you
But on and on to win the cup
Your old life and self is ***dead and gone*** ...
You've given it up
You've given it up.

I'm really keen to do things
I've got my week mapped out
Monday nights we meet for prayer
Whilst Tuesday's we're out and about
In the district doing door to door
Meeting people whose lives need changing
Some of them are very nice ...
Whilst others bang their doors
And start ranting and raving
I'm glad tonight is Wednesday
The *one* night I can *stay in*
Oh dear! I'll have to check with our Leader
To see if that thought's a sin!
I shared with a man I respect, tonight
How for a cigarette I *craved*
He said that they're not good for you
Especially when you're saved
So I'm giving them up
I'm giving them up.

Saturday *used* to be the day
I took a walk down to the park

And there I used to meet my mates
And have a natter and a bit of a lark
But these days it seems that we've lost touch
Their lives didn't mingle with mine
And since I've become a Christian
Well, I simply don't have the time
For things so unimportant
Like looking up old friends
And if you could only hear them talking
About the latest fashions and latest trends
You'd see why I made my decision
To give them up
To give them up.

A year has come and gone now
Looking back and taking stock
I've *gained* so many new things...
But *I've given up a lot!*
Still ... I've no time to ponder further
I'm going out to tea
You know ... one where you all take a dish
And it's divided ... *equally!*
I never seem to get a slice of what I took along
I've got Mrs So and So's *quiche* again
Which always turns out wrong
I used to like that girl sitting over there
She helped me give up swearing
But lately she's got on my nerves
I can't help but start comparing
Her life isn't any better than mine
Who does she think she is anyway
And I didn't think when becoming a Christian
There'd be such a price to pray
I'm getting rather weary of this Christianity
There never seems a moment
It's taking it out of me
I don't hunger for the old life ...
But I can't cope with the new
So I'm giving it up
I'm giving it up.

It's been a month now since I've been to Church
I don't feel any better
I wonder if they're missing me?
Perhaps I'll write a letter
Telling them of how I feel
And why I made my choice
But since that day I stayed away
There's been this nagging little voice...
... on and on inside my head, saying
'I'm *not* giving you up
I'm *not* giving you up
I'm *not* giving you up!'

6

Be Sure Your Sins Will Find You Out

Confession, we're told, is good for the soul. Following the humbling of myself contritely on these pages, I reason that mine should be totally restored ... as if I'd taken a walk by still waters.

'What was your inspiration to write it?' succeeded by **'have you always found it easy?'** were two of the questions I was most frequently asked, following **'An Evening With Mary'**, a forum for reciting my poetry. So dear reader, for your information, the answers.

It was a compelling creative urge on a wet Monday in 1987, and no!

How I would love to regale you with tales of the unearthing of a special talent from the day I was born, but no such attributes defined my infancy. No, I had to dig very deep before inspiration came, and like all excavations uncovered a mass of rubble in the process.

Let me take you back to when I was 12 years old, and so begin my penitent outpourings. My sisters Jean and Pearl were by now married, and they would come home to visit most Friday nights. Excitement was never far from our door, thus in a manner consistent with this, we would spend these evenings pursuing various activities such as playing board games or 'I-Spy'. Occasionally, to top that, we would engross ourselves in a poetry evening, where a topic was decided upon, and a challenge set, to see who could pen the wittiest, the longest or most inspirational poem.

By far the most **memorable** one for me has to be one of my eldest sister's efforts, as all these years later I remember it vividly. The subject chosen was zoos, and whilst the rest of us were deperately trying to wax lyrical, Jean had summed up her feelings in two concise sentences...

> Zoos are very smelly places
> Exhibiting lots of ugly faces!

My sentiments exactly, and although no prizes for length, that night all the accolades belonged to Jean.

My efforts, it has to be said, were always feeble, and since desire often precedes achieving a measure of success, I felt I was doomed. When one day I was set homework at school to write a poem based on Aesop's Fable – 'The Lion and The Mouse', I was fraught. I could not do it. Inspiration had gone AWOL.

> There once was a mouse
> Who lived in a house...

being the sum total of my toil.

Consequently it was most fortuitous for me that that night just happened to be a night when my sister Pearl was visiting. She was, and is, very good at writing poetry, and so I commandeered her help. Very quickly my homework began to take shape. It would have materialised sooner, had it not got to look like **I** had written it – too good, and it would lose authenticity!

To a certain extent, we must have accomplished our mission, as **I** only received 7 out of 10 for it, but I did get a Merit Card. And that ... I thought, was that.

The weeks passed uneventfully, until the day my English teacher called me to her desk and informed me that **my** poem had been selected to appear in a school publication which was to be distributed in the locality. I managed a look of surprised humility, and then allowed the knowledge of the distinction to be imminently conferred upon me, to trouble me no further.

During my school-days a good deal of time was spent standing **outside** the classroom. Not because the corridors held any intrinsic fascination for me, but because I couldn't behave myself **inside** the classroom. When one day I found myself again staring at the corridor wall, and a boy approached without any prior warning to take me to the Headmaster, I was somewhat concerned. Put another way, I was petrified.

Entering his study in fear and trepidation, I was surprised to be greeted by the Headmaster smiling warmly with outstretched hand ready to shake mine.

'Do come in Mary,' he gushed, 'and let me introduce you to Major-General Fortescue-Smythe.' Only at this point did I become aware of the rather important looking gentleman seated behind him.

Sheer relief that I wasn't there for disciplinary action (if I was it was taking a rather unusual form), made me relax and forget to wonder what I **was** there for. My relief however, was short-lived when the Head explained that the Major-General had seen my brilliant poem in the school magazine, and was extremely impressed.

There was more!

Impressed that one so young should disclose such talent, he wanted to award me a prize. Although, there was just **one** point he wanted to verify before we proceeded.

Was it all **entirely** my own work?

Well ... put like that, what **could** I say?

'Yes, absolutely ... I wrote it all by myself!'

We stood and beamed at each other for what was but a matter of seconds, though seemed an eternity, and then I was dismissed.

The Major-General had agreed to deliver the prize to my home, and once over the initial shock of it all, I began to warm to the idea. What would my prize be? My mind was permanently occupied with different ideas, but the one thing I desperately desired, which was to have my hair straightened, was unlikely to be fulfilled I felt on this occasion.

Eventually, prize-giving day dawned, along with the realisation that I hadn't as yet informed my parents of **my** success – best for them to be told in-situ, as it happened, so to speak. The Major-General's arrival caused quite a stir as the prerequisite pleasantries were exchanged with my rather startled and diffident mother. Her astonishment could only be added to when once again the Major-General commented on my extraordinary talent. The big moment had finally arrived. Visions of me as a straight-haired Cathy McGowan look-alike wafted before me, when the Major-General's voice drifted into my consciousness.

'I hope you'll keep this for many happy years...' (six months was the maximum I could expect from a reverse perm, so what was my prize?)

'I'm delighted Mary to present to you the book ... ***Tom Sawyer!***'

Deep gratitude was dredged up from recesses, until now unacknowledged, and blighted hope was temporarily buried as I thanked the Major-General for his generosity. My immense disappointment was soon to be overridden by inordinate relief that the whole episode could now surely die a timely death.

I cannot take any credit therefore for the following poem, and I guarantee that my sister won't thank me for including it (some people are so hard to please), but I have, for this reason. There is an obvious allegory that exists between '**my brilliant poem**' and being a Christian. Feeling weak, small and insignificant isn't alien to most of us, and Jesus is a mighty King. But in spite of this, when our lives are given to God, no gift is too meagre, no talent too insignificant. Our efforts and abilities can be turned into useful tools for the building of his kingdom.

The Great And The Small

Asleep in the Jungle a Lion lay.
When a little mouse chanced to come his way
The King of the Jungle disturbed thus
Woke up and made an awful fuss.

'What use are you tiny thing
How *dare* you come and wake a King!'
His roaring frightened the little mouse so
It ran as fast as it could go.

When it recovered from its fright
It ventured out again at night
And saw the Lion once again
Trapped in a net by wicked men.

The mouse said, 'Though a tiny thing
I too can help a mighty King.'
And through the rope unceasingly
He gnawed to set the Lion free.

The Lion now more humble said
'Twere not for you, I would be *dead*
Small things no more I'll now despise
This act of yours has made me wise.'

7

Great Expectations

Would you describe yourself as an optimist or a pessimist? If you're a Christian, don't wonder for too long, as here's the rub ... you shouldn't really be either. The Bible says we're to have **faith**. In fact it exhorts us to live by it, defining it like this:

> *'To have faith is to be sure of the things we hope for, to be certain of the things we cannot see.'* (Hebrews 11:1 NIV)

I once read about a lady who worked in the Middle East as a nanny.* One day when she was driving her jeep she ran out of fuel. She recalled that she had passed a garage a little way back, so she decided to walk and fetch some petrol. The only receptacle she could find in the back of her jeep was a potty belonging to one of her charges, so she took it along with her to the garage.

On returning to the jeep, she proceeded to fill the petrol tank with some difficulty. She became aware that she was being watched by some wealthy Arab oil sheiks, parked nearby in their Cadillac. One of them approached her and said...

'Madam, though we obviously do not share your religion, we greatly admire your faith!'

Whether or not we're Christians, most of us find it easier to talk at length pessimistically, be it about the weather, our health, or our jobs. So we do – without raising many objections. Yet talking confidently of having faith in **one**

---

* Originally read in *Pass the Port*, a collection of after-dinner stories published by Christian Brann Ltd.

God, in this age of pluralism, is tantamount to still believing the Earth is flat.

Can you imagine therefore, the biblical character Noah's predicament, when he had to try and justify his actions?

> 'I've already explained numerous times, God told me to build a boat.
>
> I know I live in a dry and crusty desert, and no, I haven't forgotten that there's currently a hose-pipe ban in enforcement, but God said it's going to rain ... a lot.
>
> Yes, it's true it hasn't rained in months in these parts, but I'm positive there's some on the way ... whatever Michael Fish says!'

Noah gets another mention later on, this time in the New Testament:

'By faith Noah, when warned about things not yet seen, in holy fear built an ark to save his family.'
(Hebrews 11:7 NIV)

We know the end of the story, the rest is history. Noah had sufficient faith not to trust the weather forecast.

Perhaps we don't feel we can go to **quite** those lengths, just yet!

We all breathe in air, although we can't see it, so we **'can be certain of the things we cannot see'** in this instance. Imagine being given a huge whiff of oxygen on Sundays which had to last us through the week. We'd all agree a daily dose would be more beneficial. It makes no more sense reserving faith for Sundays, and from Monday to Saturday side-lining God and living selfishly. Equally, going to church on high-days and holidays and then expecting God to meet our demands, is akin to a Republican turning up at Buckingham Palace unannounced, and expecting to lunch with the Queen.

The daily exercise routine that I follow rigidly is fairly basic. It involves the careful opening of one eye in the morning, followed with some caution by the other. My spirit is occasionally willing, but my flesh is generally too weak to be on more than a nodding acquaintance with physical workouts. We all have our Achilles heel, so I guess this is mine, and I must resolve to do better.

Faith, as with physical exercise, builds gradually, and like a muscle does not have to be enormous **before** we exercise it. Jesus taught his disciples that nothing was impossible for them, if they had faith as small as a mustard seed (Matthew 17:20 NIV).

A pregnant woman is often colloquially referred to as 'expecting'. To expect means to look forward to, to regard as likely to happen. If I were to ask a pregnant woman the question, 'what are you expecting at the end of nine months?' it would not surprise me in the least if her somewhat perplexed answer was, 'umm – a baby!'

I expect that's the kind of **certainty** God calls faith.

I Expect

I expect it's going to rain today
I can tell as I look at the sky.
Oh, there's a bit of blue dotted here and there
But there's a black bit too – way up high.
I expect it's going to rain today
I think it's going to pour.
It's going to come down in buckets all day
And then it will rain – some more.

I expect I'm going to catch a cold
I sat next to some germs on a bus.
The germs coughed and sneezed all over me
But I didn't make a fuss.
I sat there silently fuming
As I thought of the things I couldn't do.
'Cos the cold I was now expecting
Would probably turn – to flu.

My neighbour's expecting a baby
I expect she's getting all fat.
I expect she's feeling sick – and tired
But she might get over that
I expect she's expecting a boy or a girl
Who'll scream and bawl all night.
Then sleep its little head off all through the day
And I expect she'll be looking – a sight.

Today, I'm expecting the gas man to call
I expect I'll wait in all day.
And I expect when I've given him up and gone out
He'll knock the door and then go away.
And I'll be expected to pay for the call
Although he never visited me.
And I expect on top of the hefty bill
There'll be the usual – VAT.

I'm expecting some friends to dinner tonight
I expect there'll be hues and cries.
'Cos the tender cut of beef is tough

Great Expectations 53

And the Yorkshire Pudding won't rise.
Still, I'll do Baked Alaska for the sweet
I expect to impress them with that.
But last time the ice cream melted away
And it came out soggy – and flat.

I take my driving test tomorrow
I don't expect I'll pass.
I expect I'll fail it several times
There's not much I know about cars.
I expect the man who'll sit beside me
Will find fault with all that I do.
And I expect when he says I've failed yet again
I expect he'll smile, say 'goodbye and – thank you.'

Still ... on Sunday I'll go the local church
I expect it'll do me good.
I expect they'll all be sympathetic
Like I always knew they would.
I expect we'll sing all those lovely songs
I've quite a favourite few.
But the one I like to sing the most is...
I'm expecting great things of you!

8

Gone To War – Back In An Hour

'YOUR COUNTRY NEEDS YOU!'

Lord Kitchener adopted the above slogan in an attempt to rally the troops during the first World War. Substitute the word country for church, and the phrase wouldn't disgrace any church notice-board as a means of eye-catching advertising. God needs us, as well as us needing him. The Bible refers many times to those who belong to God as his army. The dictionary defines an army like this: '**organised body of men armed for war, professional soldiers permanently in existence.**'

The principles of church could be defined in much the same way. Christians, especially new ones need to be trained, committed and disciplined – the reason, rather unsurprisingly for being called disciples! To presume we can be God's army for one hour a week on a Sunday is absolute folly.

Ephesians 6:10–12 says:

'Finally, be strong in the Lord and in his mighty power. Put on the full armour of God, so that you can take your stand against the devil's schemes. For our struggle is not against flesh and blood, but against the rulers, against the authorities, against the powers of this dark world and against the spiritual forces of evil in the heavenly realms.'

The church is in a battle, albeit a spiritual one. Why then are we so often depicted (with some justification), as not only having woolly hats on our heads, but possessing brains to match? As funny as it may sometimes be, have you noticed how the church is always ridiculed in television sit-coms?

The world laughs, and I do too, because regrettably, there's more than a hint of truth in much of the humour. Wouldn't it be nice however, just for once to see a vicar on TV who's got something resembling a brain and a personality. *The Vicar of Dibley*, which I confess to watching and mostly enjoying, has got many things in abundance, but I'm not sure how representative she is, or should be!

If we have a winning message, which we have, we ought to have winning strategies – which we often don't have. Nowadays, if politicians want to get their message across they employ 'spin doctors' to manipulate the media and us, to hearing and believing the current sound-bites of **truth**. Whilst it's true some celebrities shun the limelight, most do not, and they enlist the help of publicists to promote positive or **negative** situations. After all, isn't **all** publicity meant to be good publicity?

The church needs good communicators too, but we don't have to use spin doctors or publicists, although why not, if it's done with integrity, is in good taste and is **effective**.

God did intend his good news to be broadcast, in the main, quite differently. He gave **us** the task. Not only are we to **have** good news, we're to **be** good news ... walking, talking, publicity agents.

A fictional story illustrates how Jesus is relying on us.

Jesus had ascended into heaven after his death and resurrection.

The Angel Gabriel said to him, **'well, that's it then, the job's done, but how will people continue to know the sacrifice you've made for them?'**

Jesus replies, **'don't worry, they will. I've told my disciples and they'll pass the word around.'**

Gabriel considers this, and then asks, **'but what if they don't, what's the backup plan?'**

'I've no other plan,' Jesus explains, 'my disciples will do as I've asked ... I'm counting on them.'

Sideways Christian Soldiers!

I'm enlisting in your army Lord, I'm signing on today
And I'm not concerned about my prospects, or the hourly rate of pay
I'm enlisting in your army Lord, for you're needing fighting men
Who, when knocked down will dust themselves off, and begin to fight again
I'm enlisting in your army Lord, for there is so much to do
And at the end I know you'll say...
'I *knew* I could count on you.'

I'm enlisting in your army Lord, and soldiers must be fit
But before I start this exhausting drill, I'll rest ... for a little bit
I'm enlisting in your army Lord, I want to move up through the ranks
And for the all the effort that I put in, I don't want any thanks
I'm enlisting in your army Lord, not for me conscription
No! I'm a willing slave for you, so I'll deserve a little mention –
In the Honours List you're keeping, of the sure and dependable few
To whom you'll say on that great day...
'I *knew* I could count on you.'

I'm enlisting in your army Lord, so I'll need a uniform
For an army's got to be noticed, if it's gonna take the world by storm
The Helmet of Salvation? Oh no – I don't need anything like that
I was thinking of something a bit more ... stylish – like umm ... a navy blue peaked cap!
The Breastplate of Righteousness, the Sword of The Spirit too?

Oh good grief, what are you thinking of, whatever would I do
With things like that ... they would be no use, I'm wanting prestige and power
Don't you realise Lord, I'm serious ... this could be your finest hour
We've got to get our act together, to have a strategy that's new
You *know* you can depend on me, and Lord...
I'm counting on you.

I'm enlisting in your army Lord, let's forget the uniform
You might have a point that I can't see ... perhaps one day it will dawn
I'm enlisting in your army Lord, I'm joining the ... Professionals
I'll be starting as a Private, working up to Corporal
I'm enlisting in your army Lord, now what's the first manoeuvre?
'Cos the battle we've got to win Lord, there's no honour in being a loser
I'm enlisting in your army Lord, I'm disciplined – at my peak
Oh, I know I was late last Sunday, but I'll be on time – next week
I'm enlisting in your army Lord, do me a favour do, yes, I want to be part of a team who'll say...
'We *knew* we could count on you.'

I'm enlisting in your army Lord, I'm gonna sign on the dotted line...
Perhaps before I do that, I need a bit more time
It is a big decision, not one to be made in a rush
Although ... what I see of the Christian church, I'll hardly be killed in the crush!
I don't think I'll enlist in your army Lord, in fact I believe that I have read
That the WI are recruiting, I'll enlist with them instead
I want to enlist in your army Lord, but I must examine the risk
There won't be peace forever – I might see active service
I will enlist in your army Lord, I promise I will – one day
I'm sure you can manage without me, there's lots more to whom you can say...
'Well done, good and faithful servant, I believe I always knew
That whereas *some* would count *the cost*
I *was sure* I could count *on you!*'

9

Now Is The Time For All Good Men To Come To The Aid Of The Party

> 'The number one cause of atheism is Christians. Those who proclaim God with their mouths and deny him with their lifestyles is what an unbelieving world finds simply unbelievable.' (Karl Rahner*)

It's such a pity that one of the most off-putting aspects of Christianity for some, is **Christians**. Were we to look upon marketing Christianity as a product, it is conceivable that we might call in a top marketing company to help us refine our promotional skills. It would not surprise me in the least, if one of the first things they pointed out was that our character and lifestyle needed to match up to the things we say – possibly because Jesus said it first! Marketing was his idea long before Saatchi & Saatchi.

Promoting products at 'parties' is now a common phenomenon, and ladies at least, if not men, will be familiar with buying anything from plastic storage boxes, toiletries, jewellery to cookware at these events. It was to the latter type of party that I was invited some years ago with fairly disastrous results. My sister-in-law had assembled family and friends together in her home, to be the captive audience to a lady who could only be described as a **passionate** devotee to pots and pans – i.e. the ones she was trying to **sell**. So devout was

* From *FROGS 11* – authors Stephen Gaukroger and Nick Mercer, published by Scripture Union, 130 City Road, London EC1V 2NJ

she in her attempt to seduce and lure us into a similar fascination, that an almost awesome hush was demanded when she was talking – which was for most of the evening. As she held aforementioned pots and pans aloft for us to admire, she sought to magnetise our attention by listing the seemingly **endless** benefits of owning this cookware for ourselves. For example, as these pots were of the slow-cooking variety, they were designed to create the minimum of work, in order that we might spend more time pursuing leisure activities.

So far ... so good.

'All you have to do' our demonstrator ebulliently gestured, 'is pop your potatoes into the pan, and leave them on a low heat whilst you go to the beach, read a book or whatever.' In due course, out came 'cooked to perfection **boiled** potatoes,' or, as she went on to reiterate, 'pop your potatoes into the pan, leave them on a low heat whilst you go...' she might well have added, 'seek extra employment,' as these pans were inordinately expensive. But hey! they were worth it, as you could also have 'cooked to perfection **roast** potatoes' ... she said.

It was amazing, it did indeed seem very simple. How had I managed without them?

There was just one thing bothering me, and I for one felt I needed some clarity on it. When she momentarily paused (she'd been on a bit of a verbal run prior to this), I drew courage, and tentatively raised my hand to obtain her attention. Having succeeded in doing so, I proceeded with my question which was...

'How does the pan **know** whether you want roast or boiled?'

Well, you could have cut the atmosphere with a knife – had they been on sale that night. The way she glared in my direction, left me in no doubt what **she** thought of my question, whilst the hysterical laughter from the other 'captives' informed me of their response. Later, they were to confess that they also had wondered, but had been too **afraid** to ask! She rather patronisingly emphasised that **obviously** you either put a little **water** in the pan for boiled, or a little **oil** for roast.

Ouch! Yes, even for me, the explanation was without ambiguity, and with hindsight (where is it when we need it?), rather obvious – but not when you've been whipped up into a frenzy beforehand with the somewhat misleading enticement that these pans were totally new and different.

For whatever reason, maybe it was something stemming back from her childhood, but this lady had clearly had a sense of humour by-pass. She was extremely frosty towards me for the remainder of the evening, as I suspect she believed I had been **deliberately** gullible and naive – which I hadn't. The situation was only exacerbated by my sister Sarah's inability and failure to refrain from erupting into paroxysms of laughter whenever she thought about how the pan knew whether we wanted roast etc., etc. This was in stark contrast to the considerable earnestness that our Sales lady was seeking to dignify the occasion with, and the **frosty** glares turned decidedly **icy**. My poor sister-in-law Doreen, who was the host, sought desperately to regain control, but to no avail. With few options left open to her, having issued several warnings, she ejected my giggling sibling from the party for bringing the whole serious nature of selling pots and pans into disrepute!

Suffice it to say ... I didn't buy a pan. What should have been a fun evening, wasn't. The seller had ostracised most of her audience with her self-centredness. We could no longer hear what she was saying about the marvellous benefits of the product, because her attitude was shouting too loudly at us, drowning it out!

Hyacinth Bucket (pronounced Bouquet!) is a character most of us have become familiar with in the TV sit-com *Keeping Up Appearances*. She is the host at parties of quite a different nature – dinner parties, more commonly known as her 'candle-light suppers', although **common** and Hyacinth are not exactly synonymous! These were occasions to be avoided at all costs by the unwilling participants – those on whom she would seek to bestow an invitation, which was not dissimilar to a royal command. I reserve the right to somewhat reluctantly, sympathise with Hyacinth. Aspects of her character are revealed in **all** of us, but hopefully to a **lesser** degree!

Gerald Coates was the initiator of the Pioneer network of churches, of which I am a part, and is the Director of Pioneer Trust. He coined the phrase 'pity-parties' to describe the negative get-togethers that lamentably are evident in most churches, and probably wherever else there is a regular gathering of disparate people. These are the grumbling, moaning affairs that disparage everything and everyone. Not that we're to abandon our critical faculties as Christians, nor resist confrontation when necessary, but constant complaining born out of self-pity is contrary to the will of God, and will be dealt with harshly. Moreover, if people fail to buy the churches 'product' because they witness our hypocrisy, we shall be held responsible.

When Jesus returns, there will be a great party in heaven, to which we are all invited. The church (us), would be the biggest party-pooper of all if we fail to entice others to be guests. The apostle Peter wrote this :

'Friends, this world is not your home, so don't make yourselves cozy in it. Don't indulge your ego at the expense of your soul. Live an exemplary life among the natives so that your actions will refute their prejudices. Then they'll be won over to God's side and be there to join in the celebration when he arrives.' (1 Peter 2:11, 12; paraphrase: Eugene H. Peterson, *The Message*)

For Pity's Sake!

I'm having a Pity Party – I hope you can attend
I'd prefer that you came on your own, but if you want to – bring a friend.
That's if you have a friend of course – I've only one or two
Perhaps *friend's* an exaggeration, I think the word acquaintance would do.

So, as I say, I'm having a Pity Party, starting punctually at eight
We'll need lots of time if we're to share, our disillusions to date.
Top of the agenda is an important subject that happens to be
Coincidentally starting, and probably ending – with me.

I'm a subject I care a great deal about – and one that is usually ignored
Because as soon as I start talking, people generally get bored.
It's as if they believe that what I have to say is of no consequence
And I know as they *pretend* to listen, their tedium is obvious and immense.

So, dear recipient of this invitation, will you respondez sil vous plais?
And not ignore me as you did on purpose when I saw you out the other day.
Oh I know you saw me coming and deliberately passed by on the other side
I would have told you how depressed I was, but again I was denied.

So, I'm having a Pity Party, to encourage others to be
More public with their dissatisfaction, and to moan more easily.

Now Is The Time... To Come To The Aid Of The Party

It's something I'm quite good at, though I wouldn't wish to boast
But when I hold my Pity Parties, I make a pretty excellent host.

I strictly limit the numbers, thereby securing the best
I wouldn't want *satisfied* people, spoiling it for the rest.
Satisfaction is a weakness and is to be deplored
It's something that I'll never be – of that, you can rest assured.

Resting, since I've mentioned it, is something I never do
I'm always rushing here and there, being one of the faithful few.
So I'm having a Pity Party to air simplistically...
That others get their act together, 'cos they're out of step with me.

I've reluctantly invited Steve, who's the life and soul and constantly witty
Thankfully, he's not coming, but I said, 'what a pity!'
You definitely don't want *humour* if the party is to succeed
To perfect the art of self-pity, it's the last thing that you need.

I think my party's timely – things have been going downhill of late
But I seem to be the only one who's worried about the state...
Our church is in ... but then I warned them, didn't I?
When they picked our pitiful leader, that they could wave success goodbye.

I wasn't even considered for the local leadership team
Even though I've sat in the front row for weeks, wearing a permanent, sanctified beam
Nodding approval, and voicing *'Amen!'* to everything our leader has said.
Yet still she overlooked me and picked someone else instead.

When the party's over, and it's time to call it a day
When we've spoken the truth ... *in love* of course ... we can all go home and pray.
For the people we're so concerned for, our motives ... never in doubt
It's the real reason for our gathering, what the party's all about.

So ... I'm having a Pity Party – I do hope you can come
Without you, the proceedings won't really be much fun.
It's an over-rated pastime ... wallowing in isolation
But when others wallow with you, it's ... it's ...

SIN!!

10

This Is A Government Health Warning!

In my formative years, spiritually speaking, there was one area I was resolutely locked in the closet about – **Heaven**. A popular song of the day used to blare out on the radio ...

> 'Everyone's gonna have religion in Glory
> Everyone's gonna be singing that story
> Everyone's gonna have a wonderful time up there
>   O glory hallelujah.'

'Everyone's gonna have **religion** in Glory' the song said, and I believed it. There was quite enough **religion** for me down here thank you very much, and if one couldn't escape it, even in heaven, then I for one didn't want to go. Had I worn a hat to church, I would have kept my secret reluctance to take up residence in God's abode of supreme bliss tucked under it. God has blessed me however with reasonable acting skills, so I'd rely on them to conceal my true feelings behind an angelic facade.

'Won't it be wonderful when we all get to Glory?' exclaimed many a person to me, who'd themselves been Christians for what seemed an eternity in itself.

With a demure smile and a slow blinking of the eyes I thereby mastered the art of agreeing convincingly that indeed it would.

I couldn't give definition to my feelings then, but I now interpret **religion** as that which locks people into legalistic rules and regulations, rather than setting them free by God's grace. Religion is extremely stifling, often steeped in unreality, and about as persuasive to the unbelieving world as suggesting that Hitler was a decent chap. Had I known then that Jesus had zero tolerance for religious people (in those days they were called Pharisees), I would have outed myself a lot sooner.

We can **all** fall into the trap. By adopting religious cliches to disguise trivial decisions, we believe it will add gravitas to our oft-times dubious judgements. Feeling led, is for some the most over-used phrase, thus immunising against the **real** thing when God genuinely reveals his direction.

Christians can be prone to 'feel led' about a multitude of things – feel led to join a church, feel led to a position of office within it, feel led to voice opinions freely, but rarely feel led to clean the loos. Occasionally they can even feel led to marry a certain person, despite the would-be recipients of their affections not **feeling led** in quite the same way! Having been led down every avenue imagineable, they can then feel led out of your church to join another.

Religion should carry a **'Government Health Warning'** – as with cigarette smoke, breathing in somebody else's religious hot air can have a serious effect, and emissions of felt-led poisoning are equally damaging. It's anti-social behaviour that alienates people, rather than attracting them, and sends them running for cover.

To be identified and pigeon-holed by one's religious denomination can be equally frustrating. When I was about to give birth to one of our three children, my husband drove me to the local hospital. Upon booking in at reception we were asked:

'What's your religion?'

My heart sank. I knew what was coming, and could sense impending delay to my increasingly essential need and desire for a bed.

'We're Christians' said my husband, with a look on his face that conveyed an innate conviction that this answer would not be satisfactory.

He was right.

'That's as maybe' said the disinterested questioner, **'but what's your *religion*?'**

'Our *religion* is *Christianity*' said my determined hubby.

'Catholic, C of E or Other!' said the speaker, her voice betraying a hint of, I'm beginning to get more than a little annoyed with this nutter!

'**Can't we *just* be Christians?**' responded my equally, I'm not going to give way on this one, husband.

By this time I was into a good deal of heavy breathing ... from exasperation. Maybe a prospective bundle of ... feeds, dirty nappies, sleepless nights, endless expense and unmitigated joy waiting to come into the world, might have had **something** to do with it!

We'd got to ... '**It's for the purposes of our form, so if anything should happen we...**' that I interjected with...

'**We're *Baptists*.**'

Relief from the receptionist, and a 'what did you go and say that for?' **look** from my husband.

In a short while I was delivered of a beautiful baby daughter whom we named Esther. It takes considerably longer to deliver people of religiosity.

Jesus **wasn't** religious. He repeatedly eschewed pious practice, and exposed the hypocrisy of his fiercest critics – those who presented a righteousness outwardly, but inwardly were full of wickedness. He enjoyed an intimate relationship with his Father in heaven – so intimate that he called him '**Abba**' meaning **Dad** or **Daddy**. Jesus referred to himself and his Father as one (**John 10:30 NIV**), and explained to his disciples that anyone who had seen him had seen the Father also.

My own Dad taught me so much about a father's love. Bringing up a family of nine children wasn't easy, but Dad (and Mum) always loved us. When, as an adult, I became more involved in church leadership, he and my mother enjoyed coming to hear me speak. A few years ago I was invited to a meeting one Saturday morning in March, and my Dad came along to listen. My subject that morning was '**Jonah**', the purpose being to emphasise God's love and compassion. Whilst driving home together my Dad conveyed to me how much he'd appreciated what I'd had to say. We said an affectionate goodbye to one another as always, but just before I drove away, Dad leaned through the window and said...

'**Bye love, I was really proud of you today.**'

It was to be the last time I would see him alive. Three days afterwards he died quite suddenly and unexpectedly of a heart attack. Whilst devastated at losing him, I was comforted by an absolute certainty that I would see him again. Dad knew Jesus as his Saviour, and he'd gone to be with him in heaven.

Jesus told his disciples before he left them, that he was going to prepare a place (heaven) for them. Because of my relationship with my Dad, I want to be with him in heaven. All my misgivings about eternity have eroded over the years, because I know and love more deeply my heavenly Father.

Heaven will be **exciting**... because God is there!

Maybe I'm still not booking early to avoid disappointment, but I'm positive heaven contains **no *religion***, and confident that as the song says...

'Everyone's gonna have a wonderful time up there!'

There's One More Annie In Heaven

My friend Annie's going to heaven, she tells me *every* day
The place is so inviting – she's practically on her way.
To be amongst things celestial, seems to be going to her head
You see – I don't think she's quite comprehended, that to go there you've got to be *dead!*
Oh – I don't mean to sound flippant or frivolous, but I really do enjoy life
And to hear Annie going on about it, it's endless toil and strife.
She says – well she says, that if we're able to endure, you know, kind of *hang on* 'til the bitter end
And not get involved in this wicked world, nor follow its fashions and trends
We'll get our reward in the great hereafter, which all seems a bit grim to me
All this enduring and hanging on, for boring perfection ... *ETERNALLY!!*
Of course! You're not meant to *enjoy* life, you must always be humble – not proud
And on Sundays, go to church several times in a day, where if you've got more than two – that's a crowd!
Annie thinks she is worthless – a miserable sinner, saved by grace.
Well, the *miserable* bit is true at least, I can tell that much by her face.
Annie's not liked much round these parts, she's called 'a Holy Joe'
She get's up peoples' noses, and nobody wants to know
What Annie's so *eager* to tell them, about being born again.
They take one look at Annie's life, and say *once* is enough ... for them.
She wants to spread her message, to others who live in the road

For them to take up their cross and help her, to carry the heavy load.
She doesn't really mix well, 'cos we're in the darkness, and she's in The Light...
It's a shame about that bit really ... she missed a right good do the other night!
Fred, her next door neighbour, often shocks her with words of abuse.
'Annie' he shouted the other day, 'you're so *!**!* heavenly minded, you're no *!**!* earthly use.'
Oh, he really got quite rattled, he worked up quite a fizz
And told her to go to a certain place, to find out how far it is.
I felt so sorry for Annie, she went a deathly white
I thought ... if she's not careful, she'll be on her way tonight!
Annie shocks so easily – she's not *of* this world, you see
Well, she's *in* it, not *of* it, and aiming to *leave* it, but speaking personally...
If I could only *believe* in God, he'd be different from Annie's for sure.
But then, my sort of God just wouldn't exist, so he's not worth looking for.
My God ... well my God would be more like a *Father*, who wouldn't frown on all that I've done
And he'd give me feelings of self-esteem, and life could still be good fun!
My God would have time to enjoy gardening, he'd want me to enjoy good health
And he wouldn't mind if I wasn't poor, so long as I didn't crave for wealth.
My God would like good music, without an organ stop in sight
And as long as I'm truly sorry, when I'm bad, he'd make me feel right.
I wouldn't feel I had to be eager, to leave this world in indecent haste
And to stay here awhile and enjoy things, would not be seen as a waste.
My God would say there's nothing that I can do to earn a place with him

And if it's good enough for him – then it's good enough for me, just to repent from my sin.
Serving him would be a *pleasure*, and something I'd *gladly* do
'Cos he'd know then how much I loved him, and *my* God...
WOULD LOVE ME TOO!!
But then, all that doesn't sound like *RELIGION*, it's so much more complex than that
Why, Annie's nearly excommunicated if she forgets to wear her hat!
Oh – that's enough about my friend, running the loser's race
And if – by chance – heaven *does* exist, I'm sure by now, she's *earnt* her place.
As I said, I don't believe in God, he's an enigma – a mystery
But if ... if my sort of God really *could* exist, I hope he'd reveal himself to me.
I'd then be in a sort of dilemma, the final irony resting with me
You see – once I'd discovered *MY* God, I couldn't wait to share him ... with Annie!

11

Spiritual DIY

I began married life in 1970 in one room on the Isle of Wight – and was thoroughly miserable.

Leaving behind my large and loving family, I felt completely isolated. With no ready-made friends on the Island, and a home so small, had I owned a cat I would never have dared swing it, as all breakages had to be paid for in rented accommodation.

Paul, my husband, was in his first teaching post, and though I'd so recently promised for better or worse, richer or poorer, at this moment in time **or** seemed the all important word – it held promise of an alternative.

Being unemployed at this time, having left my job on the mainland, I had many hours alone to fill. Frequently I'd cast my mind back to Paul's marriage proposal. Our hopes had been hinged on the fact that whilst the early years would undoubtedly be a struggle, in ten years Paul hoped he would be earning £2,000 per annum. So 1980 definitely proffered something to look forward to!

For four months we struggled to keep our financial heads above water, but a deluge of bills kept arriving and so we swam towards the mainland.

Thereafter, 'home' was with Paul's parents, until we were able to rent a tiny cottage in the same area I had lived prior to our marriage. Here we stayed for two years saving as much of our income as we were able, as a deposit on our own home. We closed our eyes to the inadequacies of our cottage – the yukky blue gloss paint on most of the walls, leading to black mould appearing because of a condensation problem. The old horse-hair sofa, full of holes with its contents protruding.

Carpets unfitted, torn and frayed. All of this could be ignored, because we had a dream before us of one day owning a nicer home. We were just extremely grateful to God, and for the kindness of our landlord who lived next door, not to mention the fact that we had a home to ourselves again.

Grateful that is, until on one particular occasion when I was made aware of how ashamed of it I could be. Since leaving the Isle of Wight I had been working for a large computer firm a few miles from where we lived. I was required to work over-time one night and as my usual lift had left earlier, my manager offered to drive me home.

As we embarked on the short journey we conversed about where I lived, what it was like, and did I enjoy living there? It appeared superfluous detail to go into the dubious attractiveness of blue gloss paint, horse-hair sofas etc. and so I didn't. But – when we were nearing our destination I began to realise that perhaps it would be only polite to invite him in for a cup of tea. After all he'd made a detour from his own journey home, it would be the least I could do. Oh dear! Suddenly, the inauspicious contents of our humble abode loomed large in my mind and I found myself fabricating, misrepresenting, evading, falsifying, dissembling (and any other word the Thesaurus can convict me with), the absolute truth. Alternatively, one could say ... I lied. I said that, stupidly, I didn't have my door key with me, and would he be so kind as to take me a few extra miles to my mother's house.

I thought then, quite wrongly I'm absolutely sure, that my manager would look down on me for not having a 'posh' house. As I recall this event, I am more ashamed now of being too ashamed to invite him into my home, than ever I could be of mere possessions.

Twenty-nine years later we are enjoying more comfortable surroundings in our current home, than ever our wildest aspirations of £2,000 per annum could have bought. Shortly after moving in, we decorated our dining room, the first room in the house to receive a face-lift. It made such a difference. It was brighter, so much more enjoyable to sit in, and therefore brought us greater pleasure.

Tossing and turning in bed one night and unable to sleep, I

decided to get up and spend some time praying instead. I made my way downstairs, but before starting couldn't resist peeking into the dining room to take another look at the fresh decor. It was to have been a **quick** peek, but I spent the night there. During the night God gave me a panoramic view of the things in my life that needed to change. The closeness to him was incredible – it was like God was in the room physically, enjoying it with me. His presence enabled me to pray for my family and friends, in a way that was fresh and invigorating, but I prayed for myself too.

It was here that I was reminded of the incident all those years ago, of being ashamed of my house. As I sat surveying the pleasing environment I realised afresh that God wanted to enjoy **living in me**, just as I was enjoying this room.

I was due for a spot of decorating.

Interior Decoration

In Father's House there's many mansions, but they need a
    lick of paint
Some, to make them like they was, and some to make them
    like they ain't!
I'm speaking metaphorically, in case you hadn't already
    guessed
I thought that bit of information I should immediately
    divest.
I'm actually talking of our bodies – though what I've gone
    and done
When I say bodies plural, is to include everyone.

You see – they are the Temples, which house the Holy
    Ghost
Though, I must say, speaking personally I've been a lousy
    host.
I've been absolutely so ashamed of how mine looks inside
I could no more invite someone else in, I've got a bit of
    PRIDE.
To do decorating properly, you need to make the room
    quite bare
To rid it of the clutter that's taken up residence there.

I've been landlord to so many things, I've a list of tenants as long as my arm
So when they demanded squatter's rights, there didn't seem any harm.
To let them stay with me awhile, I'd kick them out when I'd had enough
But they don't appear to want to leave, and the going's getting tough.
Now take my tenant *TEMPER*, he was given a long-term lease
But now I'm seeking his eviction, to give us all some peace.

BITTERNESS and *ANGER* said they would go when I gave them the boot
However, it was dangerous to give them house-room, as they've insidiously taken root.
Two of my lodgers are *SELFISH* and *IRRITABLE*, they help keep a list of what others do wrong
As my glad purveyors of *INTOLERANCE*, fools can't cross my threshold for long
I show them the door with undisguised contempt, as I fail to see their point of view
Then my tenant *CONCEITED KNOW-ALL* will say, 'you're so right, I agree with you!'

Over the years, the wear and tear gradually sets in
'Til one day you're aware that your Temple, has become the dwelling place of *SIN*.
So take time to be *HOLY*, conform yourselves to the will of God
That you may be distinguished from the unrenewed world, refined in the furnace like gold
Let God's Spirit decorate you with *LOVE*, *JOY* and *PEACE*
Be painted with *KINDNESS* and *SELF-CONTROL*
There being no law against such things, as we strive for perfection ... our goal
Take time to be holy, perfect the habit in all that you do
Thus, being transformed and reflecting *HIS GLORY*
God is pleased to dwell in his Temple ... with you.

12

Ruling Together

If you are of a certain age, you may remember a particularly amusing Morecambe and Wise sketch involving Angela Rippon. The repeat showings alone would probably ensure that everyone in the entire country has actually seen it. Following the transmission of that sketch I was inspired, much to my husband's later chagrin. Our church's Christmas party was imminent, and as we were expected to do a 'turn', I felt that Paul and myself replicating this sketch would be perfect. So replicate we did ... in all but one sense. Cast your mind back, and recall how with adroitness and great aplomb Miss Rippon (formerly only known for adding gravitas to the news), emerged from behind the newsdesk, ripping off her skirt in the process to reveal a shapely pair of legs that could also trip the light fantastic. Now I reasoned, quite correctly in my opinion, that this would be **inappropriate** for a woman in a senior position in the church ... so I **insisted** that my husband did that bit. When I emerged from behind the newsdesk, I ripped off my skirt, only to reveal another one underneath. However when Paul made his entrance, it was he who was wearing the fish-net tights.

Suffice it to say we made quite an impact!

Before your minds can conjure up images of what, it has to be said, was not a pretty sight, let me hasten to explain my reasons for telling you this.

My husband Paul and I lead a small church together, but I am the overall leader and take the bottom-line responsibility. It hasn't always been this way. Previously, Paul led the church and I was viewed as his right-hand man – or woman in this instance. Over the years we've been invited as a couple to take many meetings. In the past, a question frequently asked was, '**do you always minister together?**' I would somewhat mischievously reply, '**no, sometimes I leave Paul at home!**' The inquisitors faces were a picture, as they checked my expression, looking for evidence to convince themselves that I was probably joking. I wasn't. As in the sketch our roles have been reversed, and whilst it was acceptable for me to assist my husband, it wasn't as acceptable in many churches the other way round.

In the last decade particularly, the established Church has got itself into a right tizzy over the role of women. Men are threatening to defrock themselves if ever women are allowed to wear the trousers. Homosexual clergy and blatant disbelievers of the fundamental truths of the Christian faith, are guaranteed a safer passage to presiding over an ailing congregation, than the thought of entrusting the privilege of **serving** to a woman.

Anglicans welcomed women into the priesthood a few years ago, but the threat of division in the ranks remains. Non-conformists, including house-church, or **new** churches as we've become known, view the **priesthood** differently, but we haven't a great deal to boast about in this area either. We are doing something to rectify it however, which is better than doing nothing.

When I first became a Christian if I'd been faced with the prospect of a woman leader, pastor, minister or vicar, I would have recoiled from the very notion as much as the next man. But in those days the pastor did **everything**, and I guess I had a preference for a man to do everything, rather than a woman. Our preferences can become our prejudices and we allow our prejudices to form our theology. Increasingly churches now have leadership teams, realising that no man (or woman) can have all the gifts necessary to build a church, hence body ministry, and **the priesthood of all believers** being more than a phrase.

Jesus broke most of the rules when it came to his treatment of women. He gave them a meaningful place in Jewish society, which was hardly an equitable culture, and respected them. Rome wasn't built in a day, and neither are long held convictions and traditions changed overnight. Jesus knew that, and didn't only overturn tables in the temple, but radically overturned the minds of those who clamoured for answers when questioning his unorthodox behaviour. We've made some progress in the church in our attitudes to women. But just as we are still grappling with loving our **enemies** not simply our **friends**, turning the **other cheek** rather than **retaliating**, and executing our acts of righteousness **secretly** as opposed to **publicly**, so we must continue to keep open hearts and minds regarding the role of women.

Paul and I were married in a Baptist Church where we had met, and our Pastor and his wife **together** were responsible for leading the church. It was very new and different for us and we loved and respected them both. Inspired by them, Paul and I wanted to reflect in our wedding ceremony how **we** felt about working together, so we had a verse from the Bible inscribed inside our rings. As we exchanged our vows and our rings, we spoke this scripture to each other. It was **Psalm 34:3** (see end of poem) and fitted the bill perfectly.

The jury is still out regarding women. One day God will judge each man and each woman's work. He will test the quality of it, and if it has survived he, or she, will receive their reward.

Sounds fair to me.

Woe-Man

In the beginning God made Adam
In the beginning God made Eve
And it was never God's intention
That woman should practice to deceive
For God made her to be a companion
Intending the two to live as one
Our God then put the finishing touch
Making procreation seem like fun!

So God made Man like his Maker
Like God did God make Man
It seemed a brilliant blue-print
So what went wrong with the plan?
Woman went wrong, I hear you cry
It was woman that made it go wrong,
Poor Adam was hardly rib-tickled to death
Left to tend the land his whole life long.

'I should never have listened to you,' Adam said
*'I **knew** you'd be trouble from the start*
I don't know what I did to deserve you
We'd be better off apart.'
'If you'd have been more of a man,' Eve replied
'I'd never have bitten more than I could chew
Whatever could God have been thinking of
*The day He lumbered me with **you!**'*

So, maybe here we have the beginning
Of a pattern now set for life
For how could man subdue the Earth
When he had enough trouble controlling his wife.
Perhaps here is where the error's arisen
For man wasn't *meant* to subdue his *wife*
But to love and to cherish as Christ loved the church
By laying down his life.

So what's in a life for a man to lay down
What's involved in dying to himself?
In loving a woman for better for worse
In sickness and in health?
And should a woman promise to obey?
Should she blindly follow her man?
Let's go right back to the beginning
And discover God's *original* plan

God had destined it wouldn't be good
For man to live in isolation
So woman was formed out of Adam's rib
To his delight and delectation!
'Aha! This is more like it,' Adam exclaimed
'With birds and bees the Garden is full
*But for a **companion** as God had in mind*
*She's **much** more suitable!'*

'Now rule and reign together,' said God
'You're master of all you survey.'
And as it was written, so it was done

As evening passed, and morning became day.
The rest is history, we know the tale
Of how poor gullible Eve was led
By the cunning wile of the serpent
To question what God had said.

And man has questioned ever since
The rights of woman in this and that.
Should woman be allowed to speak in church?
And should she wear a hat?
Can we permit her to hear from God?
Can we trust her intuition?
Let's stick her in the Sunday School
And give men the important positions.

I'm not speaking of Liberation
Of burning the unmentionable thing
But of breaking down barriers we *all* have had
In our stereo-typical thinking.
And God's not a chauvinist either
By giving responsibility to the men
He made them liable to give account
Giving so many marks out of 10!

And if they're superior autocrats
Then they'll come bottom of the class
Turning the very *best* that God had in mind
Into a feudal farce.
Thus, the Battle of the Sexes
Found its place in history
Will the church have the courage to change its course?
And by the church I mean...
You and *Me!*

Or will we stick doggedly to the dogma
Afraid to take the chance
Turning God's oportunity into a threat
Lest women may enhance
The areas where purely men have trod
Not by *destiny*, but by default
Hence the Spirit whispers in the ears of men
'It's time to call a halt.'

For He made us *all* the sons of God
And whilst the enemy has sought to deceive us
He's robbed women of their rightful place
In the *Priesthood of all Believers*.
No longer *Jew* or *Greek*
No longer *Slave* or *Free*
No longer *Men* or *Women*
But believers in *Unity*.
'By this, shall all men know that you are my disciples
Love being the greatest commandment ever.'
So Magnify the Lord with me
And let us exalt His Name ... *Together!* (Psalm 34:3)

13

Go Ahead Caller – You're Through

I started this book by asking the question can we speak to God, and if so, does he listen?

I'll finish by asking can God speak to us? I believe he can – and does, though the problem so often is – **we're** not listening!

When I first wrote these poems, I decided to give them an airing, to see how they would be received. It was to be a singularly auspicious occasion entitled, '**An Evening with M.A.R.Y.**' – Mary being an acronym for **M**ainly **A**necdotes, **R**hymes and **Y**awns ... sorry, Yarns! Family, friends, neighbours and complete strangers were present, and it seemed to go well and was considered successful. I was pleased. Well I was, until the next day, when I stood at the kitchen sink (like you do) analysing its merits.

Had they **really** enjoyed it?

Doubt it, came the booming reply in my head.

Hadn't I conveyed some rather foolish things about myself?

You sure did, came the **immediate** confirmation.

Should I ever do anything like this again?

Only if you **don't mind** *looking foolish*, came the somewhat predictable reply.

Oh, how embarrassing. What had I done? In front of all those people too. How could I have been so naive? These thoughts, and a few dozen more, were whirling round and round in my mind until finally my confidence was, so to speak, down the plug-hole along with the dirty washing up water.

And my response?

Here I Am Lord ... Send Him!

You see, Satan can also speak to us. Being the very antithesis of God he sows seeds of failure, humiliation, doubt and despair. When, by crushing our spirits and destroying self-esteem he prevents us from doing something, he's succeeded – that's exactly what he wants – to immobilise us. It's the work of Satan to accuse. It's the work of the Holy Spirit to convict – a **big** difference. Satan will tell us we'll never be **good enough**. The Holy Spirit will show us where we're going wrong, yet convince we'll never be **bad enough** for God to stop loving us and using us.

My husband Paul was not brought up in a church-going family, nor did they claim to believe in God, so unlike myself he had no childhood experience of Sunday School or Church. When he was a young boy, finding a Bible in the bookcase, he opened it up and began to read it. With most books you usually start at the beginning, and since this seemed reasonable to him, that is what he decided to do. Perhaps with hindsight, this was rather unwise, as he found himself bogged down in people sacrificing animals and such to God. Undeterred, he decided that as he had a bag of sweets, why not 'sacrifice' one of these? Putting it on the window-sill he told God that he could eat it, it was his.

Curiosity, as well as a desire to eat the sweet himself (his earlier benevolent intentions having temporarily been sidelined), prevented him from waiting **too** long for God to act. Every so often therefore, he would check the situation.

Perhaps God hasn't got a sweet tooth, possibly he's more into savouries. Finding the sweet still on the window-sill after a decent length of time had elapsed was, in in this little boy's estimation, total justification for his following action. Yielding to the temptation before him, he gobbled the sweet with an '**OK God, so you didn't want it!**'

Years later, when he became a Christian, he was reminded of this incident and felt God was saying to him, 'I didn't want your **sweet** Paul ... I wanted **you!**'

The prophet Isaiah knew God wanted him in a similar way, if only being slightly more dramatic in the telling of the event, which we can read about in the book of **Isaiah Chapter 6**. He was in the temple when the glory of God suddenly filled it with his presence, and he heard God asking *'who will be my messenger?'* Isaiah was eager to respond, *'send me Lord.'*

When the government wanted to alert us to the issue of **AIDS**, a decade or so ago, they launched a campaign that they hoped would grab our attention. As this is a killer disease they tried to ensure the slogan would have maximum impact. Hence **'AIDS – DON'T DIE OF IGNORANCE'** filled our television screens, billboards and other advertising mediums for months.

God doesn't want us to die of ignorance either, and he wants to communicate how we don't need to – if we'll listen.

The church is not a building, it's people, and we are God's messengers. We are his campaign idea, we are the slogan that should catch the attention of the world. We were destined to die because of sin, but God sent his son into this world to die for us. Jesus took all the things **we've** done wrong upon **himself**, so that when we are truly sorry we are forgiven.

The church has a major role to play in society, it's not redundant. Its voice must be heard – clearly.

To quote Gerald Coates (and why not, as Barry Norman would say, or is it Rory Bremner?), he says that if our target is to aim at nothing, we will probably hit it! In archery terms, if your arrow falls short of the target, you are told you have 'sinned'. The Bible says that we have **all** fallen short of God's glory (**Romans 3:23**), which is the standard of God alone, and in contrast to that, none of us measure up. It is only through his grace, meaning '**undeserved favour**', that we are justified. I was taught as a child to remember the meaning of that word like this – 'just as if I'd never sinned'. So none of us are perfect, including Christians in the church ... but we are forgiven.

God is still looking for people who will, like the prophet Isaiah, 'go' for him.

Margaret Thatcher once memorably declared, **'U-turn if you want to, but the lady's not for turning!'**

This lady (me), however, made a promise to God, as I stood at the kitchen sink that morning. Doing a complete U-turn or U-bend, from my previous negative thoughts, back through the plughole, I felt inspired to 'go' for God, and also to write another poem.

Here I Am Lord – Send Him

In the year that King Uzziah died, Isaiah saw the Lord
He was high and lifted up and exalted, and His Glory filled the world!
The Temple shook to its very foundations, the Sanctuary was filled with smoke
And Isaiah aware of his sinfulness, felt doomed in a world without hope.
But in Isaiah's vision, a creature carried a burning coal
And placing it on Isaiah's lips pronounced, 'No longer guilty, you're now made whole.'
Then the Lord was heard to ask, 'Who will be my messenger, who shall go, who will it be?'
So Isaiah responded eagerly...
'Here I am Lord, send me.'

Before anything else existed, there was Christ with God
And the Prophet John in the wilderness cried...
'Prepare ye, the way of the Lord!'
The glory that was his with the Father, in humility Christ left it behind
To make the ultimate sacrifice, by dying for all mankind.
And the world's foundations shook that day, as he paid the price for our sin
But our guilt would have remained, if that day he'd said...
'Here I am God, send him.'

The year is 1999, Elizabeth is our Queen
And the harvest is as ripe as it's ever been, but the workers are few and far between
And the Church's foundations are shaking, as they've never shaken before
And the ill at ease doctrinally are being challenged to the core
As we defend the indefensible, God's voice is growing more dim

As in apathy and complacency, we respond...
'Here I am Lord, send him.'

So Christians awake! Salute this happy morn
Arise now from your sleepful state, for the church must be reborn
It's time for us to take our place, amongst minorities
Whose voices are the loudest heard, so that influence rests with these
Who else should we blame for the chaos? Have we reason to condemn?
If our response to God's clear calling is...
'Here we are Lord, send them.'

Don't let's be resigned to our weakness, for in our ignorance we're made wise
For God sent the fools to set the captives free, and the dim to give sight to blind eyes
So Christians, let's begin *shouting*, let's stamp our feet with the rest
And get in the ring where the fighting is, and like true champions, show we're the best!

For God's fighting with us in our corner, and when we're
    seconds away from the bout
He'll whisper words of encouragement, eliminating all our
    doubt
And though our bodies may be shaking, convinced of how
    pathetic we shall be
Our timid voices should be heard to declare...
'If you really think I'd be some use, then
Here I am Lord ... please ... send me!'

14

A Final Word

It had been a good meeting, the presence of the Lord had been unusually evident. God had spoken to us. Although it was the leader speaking, I had clearly recognised it as God's voice.

First and foremost, he had reminded us of how much he loved us, but we had some growing up to do. Some were likened to ten-year-old spiritual babies! My mind had wandered. Years ago, when embarking on church leadership, I had been asked what my burden for the church had been, and it was precisely that ... to see it grow up in Christ.

Hebrews 5 and 6 exhorts us to leave the elementary teachings about Jesus, reminding us that milk is for newborn babies, and to go on to solid food which is for the mature. I could hear the speaker tell us that we were living in times when God would be accelerating the things that he did. I could **hear** what he was saying.

Thirty years ago when I was a teenager there weren't as many motorways as there are today, and most journeys took a lot longer. Nearly all our family 'bangers' which we were privileged to own, necessitated us taking the scenic route! As I look back through the pages of this book, I appreciate that many readers may not relate to what I've written because for them, their experience of being 'church' has never been like that ... Praise the Lord!

Whilst others may be thinking ... what's changed?

Learning from our past mistakes, as well as our present ones, is essential. I'm deeply indebted to **all** the people who've had input into my life. Those who laid the foundations when I was younger, enabling me to build on them to today, with the people I currently trust to keep me on the straight and narrow.

British Rail, used to have a slogan **'We're getting there'**. The fact that they are no longer in existence perhaps indicates they didn't get there quickly enough. When I started to lead a church many years ago, I confused God with British Rail, and was somewhat anxious about 'getting there' ... wherever **there** was. Because God isn't only concerned with us arriving, he answered that anxiety in this way.

'Mary,' he said, 'I want you to *enjoy* the journey!'

Since then I've always **tried** to.

So as I'd sat in the meeting, pondering the significance of what God had said, echoes of my Dad's final words to me came to my mind.

'Bye love, I was really proud of you today.'

Matthew 3:16, 17 says:

> *'As soon as Jesus was baptised, he went up out of the water. At that moment heaven was opened, and he saw the Spirit of God descending like a dove and lighting on him. And a voice from heaven said, **'This is my Son, whom I love; with him I am well pleased.**'*

I resolved to accelerate the process of God, my heavenly Father, being able to affirm me in the same way – to endeavour to consistently live my life in a way that is pleasing to him.

The Holy Spirit continues to change peoples' lives, and is constantly changing the face of the church. I'm excited about that, and I aim to enjoy it.

I hope you will too ... happy travelling!